GUITAR • VOCAL

STRUM & SING   LEONARD COHEN

Cover photo: MARKA / Alamy Stock Photo

ISBN: 978-1-5400-2231-8

HAL•LEONARD®

Visit Hal Leonard Online at
www.halleonard.com

Contact us:
Hal Leonard
7777 West Bluemound Road
Milwaukee, WI 53213
Email: info@halleonard.com

In Europe, contact:
Hal Leonard Europe Limited
42 Wigmore Street
Marylebone, London, W1U 2RN
Email: info@halleonardeurope.com

In Australia, contact:
Hal Leonard Australia Pty. Ltd.
4 Lentara Court
Cheltenham, Victoria, 3192 Australia
Email: info@halleonard.com.au

CONTENTS

Anthem

Words and Music by
Leonard Cohen

(Capo 1st fret)

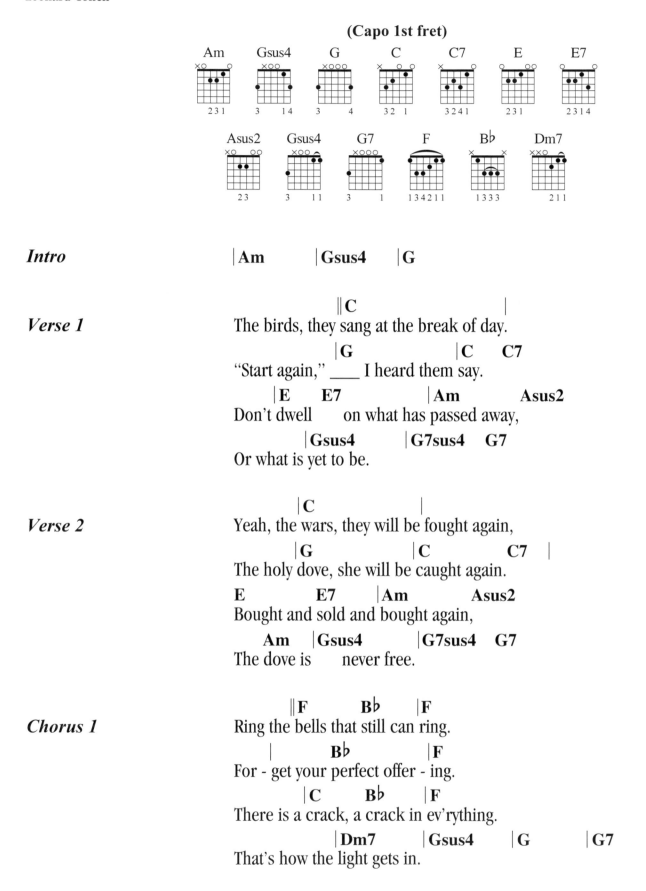

Intro |**Am** |**Gsus4** |**G**

Verse 1

‖**C** |
The birds, they sang at the break of day.
|**G** |**C**   **C7**
"Start again," ____ I heard them say.
|**E**   **E7** |**Am**   **Asus2**
Don't dwell   on what has passed away,
|**Gsus4** |**G7sus4**   **G7**
Or what is yet to be.

Verse 2

|**C** |
Yeah, the wars, they will be fought again,
|**G** |**C**   **C7** |
The holy dove, she will be caught again.
E   **E7** |**Am**   **Asus2**
Bought and sold and bought again,
Am |**Gsus4** |**G7sus4**   **G7**
The dove is   never free.

Chorus 1

‖**F**   **B♭** |**F**
Ring the bells that still can ring.
| **B♭** |**F**
For - get your perfect offer - ing.
|**C**   **B♭** |**F**
There is a crack, a crack in ev'rything.
|**Dm7** |**Gsus4** |**G** |**G7**
That's how the light gets in.

4

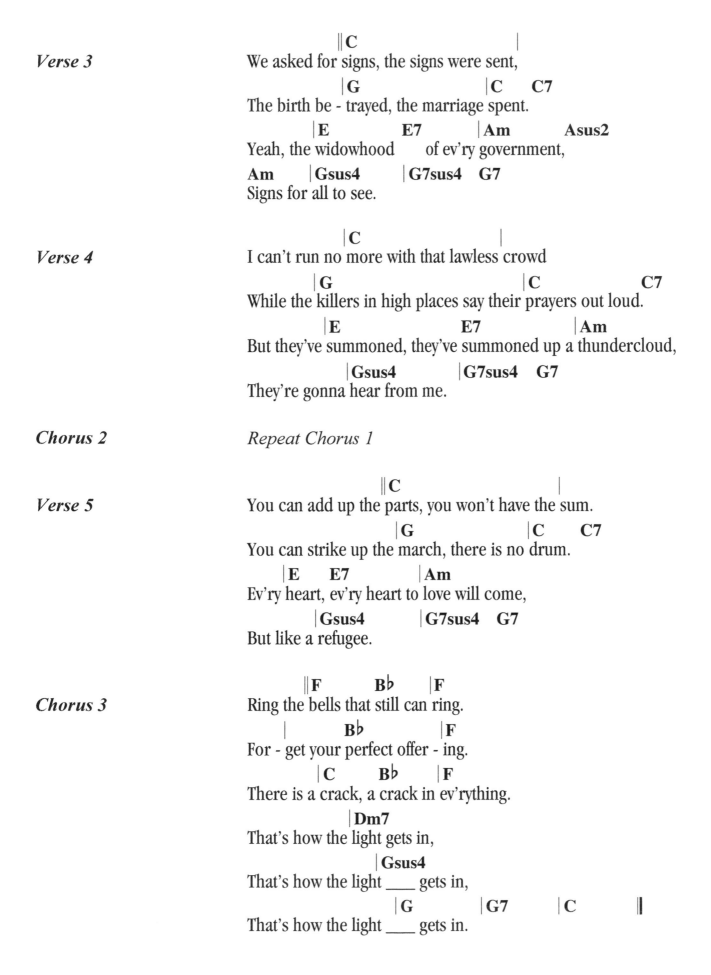

Verse 3

     ‖C |
We asked for signs, the signs were sent,
      |G |C   C7
The birth be - trayed, the marriage spent.
     |E   E7 |Am   Asus2
Yeah, the widowhood   of ev'ry government,
Am |Gsus4 |G7sus4 G7
Signs for all to see.

Verse 4

      |C |
I can't run no more with that lawless crowd
     |G |C   C7
While the killers in high places say their prayers out loud.
      |E   E7 |Am
But they've summoned, they've summoned up a thundercloud,
       |Gsus4 |G7sus4 G7
They're gonna hear from me.

Chorus 2   *Repeat Chorus 1*

Verse 5

      ‖C |
You can add up the parts, you won't have the sum.
        |G |C   C7
You can strike up the march, there is no drum.
   |E E7 |Am
Ev'ry heart, ev'ry heart to love will come,
    |Gsus4 |G7sus4 G7
But like a refugee.

Chorus 3

     ‖F   Bb |F
Ring the bells that still can ring.
    | Bb |F
For - get your perfect offer - ing.
     |C   Bb |F
There is a crack, a crack in ev'rything.
      |Dm7
That's how the light gets in,
      |Gsus4
That's how the light ___ gets in,
      |G |G7 |C   ‖
That's how the light ___ gets in.

Bird on the Wire
(Bird on a Wire)

Words and Music by
Leonard Cohen

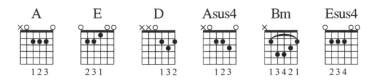

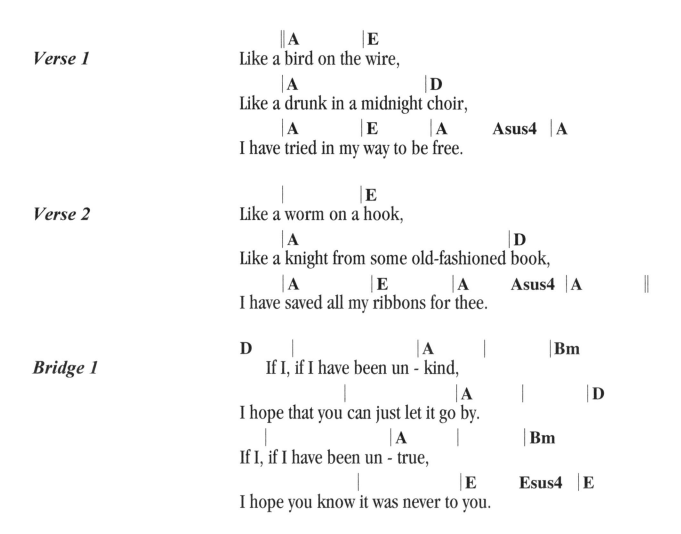

Verse 1

‖A |E
Like a bird on the wire,

|A |D
Like a drunk in a midnight choir,

|A |E |A   Asus4 |A
I have tried in my way to be free.

Verse 2

| |E
Like a worm on a hook,

|A |D
Like a knight from some old-fashioned book,

|A |E |A   Asus4 |A   ‖
I have saved all my ribbons for thee.

Bridge 1

D | |A | |Bm
    If I, if I have been un - kind,

| |A | |D
I hope that you can just let it go by.

| |A | |Bm
If I, if I have been un - true,

| |E   Esus4 |E
I hope you know it was never to you.

Verse 3

        ‖**A** |**E**
More like a baby still - born,

    |**A** |**D**
Like a beast with his horn,

    |**A** |**E** |**A**   **Asus4** |**A**
I have torn ev'ry - one who reached out for me.

Verse 4

        | |**E**
But I swear by this song,

    |**A** |**D** |**A**
And by all that I have done wrong,

        |**E** |**A**   **Asus4** |**A**   ‖
I will make it all up to thee.

Bridge 2

D | |**A** | |**Bm**
    I saw a beggar leaning on his wooden crutch.

          | |**A** | |**D**
He said to me, "You must not ask for so much."

            | |**A** | |**Bm**
And a pretty woman leaning in her darkened door,

          | |**E**   **Esus4** |**E**
She cried to me, "Hey, why not ask for more?"

Outro-Verse

        ‖**A** |**E**
More like a bird on the wire,

   |**A** |**D**
Like a drunk in a midnight choir,

   |**A** |**E** |**D** |**A**   ‖
I have tried in my way to be free.

Chelsea Hotel #2

Words and Music by
Leonard Cohen

(Capo 5th fret)

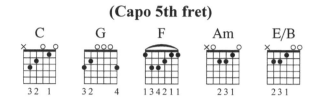

Verse 1

‖C |G |F |C
I re - member you well in the Chelsea Ho - tel,
      | |G |Am |
You were talking so brave and so sweet.
C |G |F |C
Giving me head on the unmade bed
      |F | |G |
While the limousines wait in the street.
Am | |F |
Those were the reasons and that was New York,
      |C |E/B |Am |
We were running for the money and the flesh.
   |F | |C |
And that was called love for the workers in song,
      |F | |G |
Probably still is for those of them left.

Chorus 1

      ‖F |C |
Ah, but you got a - way, didn't you, baby?
      | |E/B |Am |
You just turned your back on the crowd.
F | |C |
You got a - way, I never once heard you say,
 |F | |C |
"I need you,   I don't need you,
 |F | |C |
I need you,   I don't need you."
      |F | |Am | |G |
And all of that jivin' a - round.

```
  ‖C          |G      |F          |C
I re - member you well in the Chelsea Ho - tel,
      |              |G      |Am          |
You were famous, your heart was a legend.
      |C          |G          |F          |C
You told me a - gain you preferred handsome men
          |F          |              |G          |
But for me you would make an exception.
  |Am          |      |F          |
And clenching your fist for the ones like us
              |C          |E/B      |Am          |
Who are op - pressed by the figures of beauty,
  |F          |      |C          |
You fixed yourself, you said, "Well, never mind,
      |F      |      |G          |
We are ugly but we have the music."
```

```
          ‖F          |      |C              |
And then you got a - way, didn't you, baby?
      |              |E/B      |Am      |          |
You just turned your back on the crowd.
F          |              |C          |
You got a - way, I never once heard you say,
  |F          |      |C          |
"I need you,      I don't need you,
  |F          |      |C              |
I need you,      I don't need you."
      |F          |      |Am          |      |G          |
And all of that jivin' a - round.
```

```
          ‖C          |G      |F          |C
I don't mean to sug - gest that I loved you the best,
      |              |G      |Am          |
I can't keep track of each fallen robin.
      |C          |G      |F          |C
I re - member you well in the Chelsea Ho - tel,
          |F              |              |G      |          ‖
That's all, I don't even think of you that often.
```

Dance Me to the End of Love

Words and Music by
Leonard Cohen

(Capo 3rd fret)

Am   Em   B7   D

Intro

‖: **Am** | | **Em** | |
La, la, la, la, la, la. La, la, la, la, la, la.
B7 | | **Em** | :‖
La, la, la, la, la.

Verse 1

Am | | **Em** | |
Dance me to your beauty with a burning violin.
Am | | **Em** | |
Dance me through the panic till I'm gathered safely in.
Am | | **Em** | |
Lift me like an olive branch and be my homeward dove.
B7 | **Em** | |
Dance me to the end of love.
B7 | **Em** | |
Dance me to the end of love.

Verse 2

‖ **Am** | | **Em** | |
Oh, let me see your beauty when the witnesses are gone.
Am | | **Em** | |
Let me feel you're moving like they do in Babylon.
Am | | **Em** |
Show me slowly what I only know the limits of.
|**B7** | **Em** | |
Oh, dance me to the end of love,
B7 | **Em** | ‖
Dance me to the end of love.

Interlude 1	‖: D | |Em | :‖

Verse 3

Am | |Em | |
Dance me to the wedding now, dance me on and on.
Am | |Em |
Dance me very tenderly and dance me very long.
    |Am | |Em | |
We're both of us be - neath our love, we're both of us a - bove.
B7 | |Em | |
Dance me to the end of love.
B7 | |Em | ‖
Dance me to the end of love.

Verse 4

Am | |Em | |
Dance me to the children who are asking to be born.
Am | |Em | |
Dance me through the curtains that our kisses have outworn.
Am | |Em | |
Raise a tent of shelter now, though ev'ry thread is torn.
B7 | |Em | ‖
Dance me to the end of love.

Interlude 2   *Repeat Interlude 1*

Bridge   *Repeat Intro*

Verse 5

Am | |Em | |
Dance me to your beauty with a burning violin.
Am | |Em | |
Dance me through the panic till I'm gathered safely in.
Am | |Em | |
Touch me with your naked hand, touch me with your glove.
B7 | |Em | |
Dance me to the end of love.
B7 | |Em | |
Dance me to the end of love.
B7 | |Em | ‖
Dance me to the end of love.

Everybody Knows

Words and Music by
Leonard Cohen and Sharon Robinson

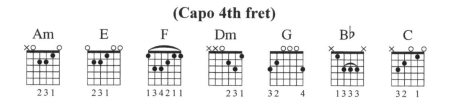

Intro |Am |E |Am |

Verse 1

‖**Am** |
Ev'rybody knows that the dice are loaded.
|**F** |
Ev'rybody rolls with their fingers crossed.
|**Am** |
Ev'rybody knows the war is over.
|**F** |
Ev'rybody knows the good guys lost.
|**Dm** |**E**
Ev'rybody knows the fight was fixed.
|**G** |**Am**
The poor stay poor, the rich get rich.
|**B♭** |**E**
That's how it goes,
|**Am** |
Ev'rybody knows.

Verse 2

   ‖**Am** |
Ev'rybody knows that the boat is leaking.
   |**F** |
Ev'rybody knows the captain lied.
   |**Am** |
Ev'rybody got this broken feeling
   |**F** |
Like their father or their dog just died.
   |**Dm** |**E**
Ev'rybody talking to their pockets.
   |**G** |**Am**
Ev'rybody wants a box of choc'lates
      |**B♭** |**E**
And a long stem rose.
   |**Am** |
Ev'rybody knows.

Verse 3

   ‖**Am** |
Ev'rybody knows that you love me, baby.
    |**F** |
Ev'rybody knows that you really do.
   |**Am** | |
Ev'rybody knows that you've been faithful,
F |
Give or take a night or two.
   |**Dm** |**E**
Ev'rybody knows you've been dis - creet,
      |**G** |**Am**
But there were so many people you just had to meet
   |**B♭** |**E**
Without your clothes.
   |**Am** |
And ev'rybody knows.

Chorus 1

```
          ‖C          |
Ev'rybody knows,
          |G          |
Ev'rybody knows
               |Am        |G
That's how it goes.
F         |C          |
Ev'rybody knows.

          |          |
Ev'rybody knows,
          |G          |
Ev'rybody knows
               |Am        |G
That's how it goes.
F         |C          |          |Am        |
Ev'rybody knows.
```

Verse 4

```
               ‖Am                    |
And ev'rybody knows that it's now or never.
          |F                      |
Ev'rybody knows that it's me or you.
               |Am            |          |
And ev'rybody knows that you live for - ever
F                      |
When you've done a line or two.
          |Dm          |E
Ev'rybody knows the deal is rotten.
          |G            |Am
Old Black Joe's still pickin' cotton
                    |Bb        |E
For your ribbons and bows.
          |Am        |
And ev'rybody knows.
```

Verse 5

```
          ‖Am                        |
And ev'rybody knows that the plague is coming.
          |F                  |
Ev'rybody knows that it's moving fast.
          |Am                        |
Ev'rybody knows that the naked man and woman
          |F              |
Are just a shiny artifact of the past.
          |Dm              |E
Ev'rybody knows the scene is dead,
                      |G            |Am
But there's gonna be a meter on your bed
              |Bb          |E
That will dis - close
                |Am        |
What ev'rybody knows.
```

Verse 6

```
                |Am              |
And ev'rybody knows that you're in trouble.
          |F                    |
Ev'rybody knows what you've been through,
                    |Am        |        |
From the bloody cross on top of Calvary
F                    |
To the beach of Malibu.
          |Dm                  |E
Ev'rybody knows it's coming apart.
              |G            |Am
Take one last look at this Sacred Heart
          |Bb          |E
Before it blows.
                |Am        |
And ev'rybody knows.
```

Chorus 2

```
               ‖ C           |
Ev'rybody knows,
               | G           |
Ev'rybody knows
                    | Am          | G
That's how it goes.
F          | C           |
Ev'rybody knows.

               |             |
Ev'rybody knows,
               | G           |
Ev'rybody knows
                    | Am          | G
That's how it goes.
F          | C           |
Ev'rybody knows.

               |             |
Ev'rybody knows,
               | G           |
Ev'rybody knows
                    | Am          |
That's how it goes.
G    F      | C           |             ‖
Oh, ev'rybody knows.
```

Famous Blue Raincoat

Words and Music by
Leonard Cohen

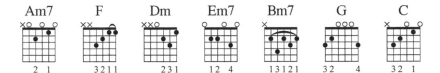

Intro

|Am7 | |F | |
|Dm | |Em7 |

Verse 1

‖Am7 | |F | |Dm
It's four in the morning, the end of De - cember,
   | |Em7 | |
I'm writing you now just to see if you're better.
Am7 | |F |
New York is cold, but I like where I'm living,
   |Dm | |
There's music on Clinton Street
Em7 | |Am7
All through the evening.
 | |Bm7 | |Am7 |
I hear that you're building your little house
   |Bm7 | |Am7
Deep in the desert.
 | |G |
You're living for nothing now.
   |Am7 | |G |
I hope you're keeping some kind of record.

Chorus 1

```
        ‖C  |           |
Yes, 'n' Jane came
           |                |G           |
By with a lock of your hair.
           |               |Am7          |
She said that you gave it to her
           |               |Bm7   |       |G       |        |F
That night that you planned to go clear.
           |          |Em7          |
Did you ever go clear?
```

Verse 2

```
        ‖Am7          |              |F            |
Ah, the last time we saw you, you looked so much older.
        |Dm           |           |Em7       |
Your famous blue raincoat was torn at the shoulder.
        |Am7          |         |F            |           |Dm
You'd been to the station to meet ev'ry train.
           |                |Em7          |
You came home without Lili Marlene.
        |Am7  |         |Bm7         |
And you treated      my woman
        |Am7  |         |Bm7     |       |Am7
To a flake   of your life.
           |                |G       |        |Am7
And when she came back,
           |          |G            |
She was nobody's wife.
```

Chorus 2

```
        ‖C  |           |
Well, I see you
           |                |G           |         |
There with a rose in your teeth,
           |               |Am7          |         |
One more thin Gypsy thief.
           |               |Bm7   |       |G       |       |F
Well, I see Jane's a - way,
           |               |Em7          |         ‖
She sends her regards.
```

Interlude

```
|Am7          |            |F           |              |
|Dm           |            |Em7         |
```

Verse 3

```
        ‖Am7      |            |F          |          |Dm
And what can I tell you my brother, my killer?
            |              |Em7        |
What can I possibly say?
     |Am7     |            |F
I guess that I miss you,
               |            |Dm
I guess I for - give you.
               |              |Em7       |            |Am7
I'm glad you stood in my way.
          |          |Bm7      |           |Am7
If you ever come by here
          |          |Bm7      |           |Am7
For Jane or for me
            |          |G        |          |Am7
Well, your enemy is sleeping
          |          |G        |
And his woman is free.
```

Chorus 3

```
            ‖C         |         |
Yes, and thanks
          |              |G   |             |           |
For the trouble you took from her eyes.
     |              |Am7  |            |
I thought it was there    for good,
      |       |Bm7      |           |G        |
So I never tried.
```

Chorus 4

```
            ‖C   |         |
And Jane came
              |              |G          |
By with a lock of your hair.
          |          |          |Am7       |
She said that you gave it to her
            |          |
That night that you planned
            |Bm7      |           |G         |           |F
To go clear.
          |          |Em7      |            ‖
Sin - cerely, L. Cohen.
```

First We Take Manhattan

Words and Music by
Leonard Cohen

(Capo 1st fret)

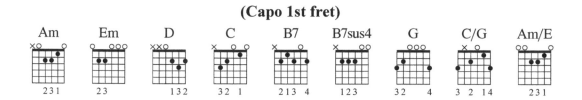

Intro

‖: Am | |Em | :‖ *Play 3 times*
|D |C |B7 | |Em |

Verse 1

‖Am | |Em |
They sentenced me to twenty years of boredom
|Am | |Em |
For trying to change the system from within.
|Am | |Em | |
I'm coming now, I'm coming to re - ward them.
D |C |B7sus4 |
First we take Man - hattan,
B7 |Em | | |
Then we take Ber - lin.

Verse 2

‖Am | |Em |
I'm guided by a signal in the heavens.
|Am | |Em |
I'm guided by this birthmark on my skin.
|Am | |Em | |
I'm guided by the beauty of our weapons.
D |C |B7sus4 |
First we take Man - hattan,
B7 |Em |
Then we take Ber - lin.

Chorus 1

```
      ‖G        |C/G  G      |D      |C
```
I'd really like to live be - side you, baby.
```
      D    |G         |C/G  G    |Em       |
```
I love your body and your spirit and your clothes.
```
           |G              |C/G   G      |Am/E  Em |
```
But you see that line there moving through the sta -   tion?
```
      |D      |C        |B7sus4    |
```
I told you, I told you, I told you
```
B7         |Em       |
```
I was one of those.

Verse 3

```
            ‖Am              |
```
Ah, you loved me as a loser,
```
                 |Em                        |
```
But now you're worried that I just might win.
```
                 |Am           |
```
You know the way to stop me,
```
            |Em          |
```
But you don't have the disci - pline.
```
          |Am         |
```
How many nights I prayed for this:
```
       |Em          |          |
```
To let my work begin.
```
D              |C       |B7sus4    |
```
First we take Man - hattan,
```
B7             |Em     |       |      |     ‖
```
Then we take Ber - lin.

Verse 4

```
Am            |              |Em       |
```
I don't like your fashion business, mister.
```
      |Am        |              |Em     |       |
```
And I don't like these drugs that keep you thin.
```
Am            |              |Em      |       |
```
I don't like what happened to my sister.
```
D            |C       |B7sus4     |
```
First we take Man - hattan,
```
B7            |Em      |      |      |
```
Then we take Ber - lin.
```
```

Chorus 2

```
     ‖G          |C/G  G        |D           |C
I'd really like to live be - side you, baby.
        D      |G            |C/G  G     |Em           |
I love your body and your spirit  and your clothes.
            |G                |C/G  G          |Am/E  Em  |
But you see that line there moving through the sta   -     tion?
|D          |C           |B7sus4       |
I told you, I told you, I told you
B7          |Em          |            |            |
I was one of those.
```

Verse 5

```
          ‖Am          |            |Em          |
And I thank you for those items that you sent me:
      |Am           |            |Em          |
The monkey and the plywood violin.
|Am             |            |Em            |            |
I practiced ev'ry night, now I'm ready
D              |C           |B7sus4       |
First we take Man - hattan,
B7                     ‖
Then we take Ber -
```

Interlude

```
|Em          |D           |C          |B7sus4      |
- lin.
```

Verse 6

```
          ‖Am          |            |Em          |
Ah, re - member me, I used to live for music,
       |Am           |            |Em          |
Re - member me, I brought your groc'ries in.
          |Am          |            |Em          |            |
Well, it's Father's Day and ev'rybody's wounded.
D              |C           |B7sus4       |
First we take Man - hattan,
B7                     ‖
Then we take Ber -
```

Outro

```
|Em          |      D |Em          |      D  |
- lin.
‖:Em         |      D |Em          |      D :‖ Repeat and fade
```

22

So Long Marianne

Words and Music by
Leonard Cohen

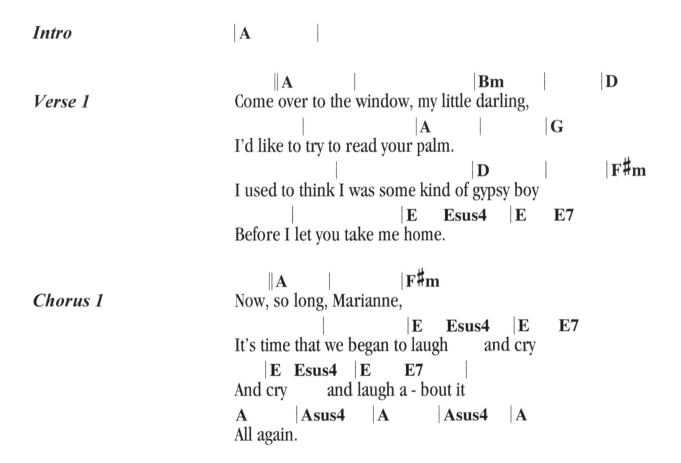

Intro |A |

Verse 1

||A | |Bm | |D
Come over to the window, my little darling,
          | |A | |G
I'd like to try to read your palm.
          | |D | |F#m
I used to think I was some kind of gypsy boy
          | |E Esus4 |E E7
Before I let you take me home.

Chorus 1

||A | |F#m
Now, so long, Marianne,
          | |E Esus4 |E E7
It's time that we began to laugh   and cry
|E Esus4 |E E7 |
And cry   and laugh a - bout it
A |Asus4 |A |Asus4 |A
All again.

Verse 2

```
              ‖A        |      |Bm           |        |D
Well, you know that I love to live with you
                         |          |A      |        |G
But you make me for - get so very much.
                 |          |D          |
I forget to pray for the angel
                 |F♯m      |            |E   Esus4  |E   E7
And then the angels for - get to pray for us.
```

Chorus 2

Repeat Chorus 1

Verse 3

```
              ‖A        |      |Bm           |        |D
We met when we were almost young
                 |          |A      |        |G
Deep in the green lilac park.
                 |          |D          |      |F♯m
You held on to me like I was a crucifix
                 |                      |E   Esus4  |E   E7
As we went kneeling through the dark.
```

Chorus 3

Repeat Chorus 1

Verse 4

```
              ‖A        |          |Bm           |        |D
Your letters, they all say that you're be - side me now.
                 |          |A      |        |G
Then why do I feel alone?
                 |              |D          |
I'm standing on a ledge, and your fine spider web
        |F♯m      |            |E   Esus4  |E   E7
Is fastening my ankle to a stone.
```

Chorus 4

Repeat Chorus 1

Verse 5

```
‖A    |        |Bm        |        |D
```
For now I need your hidden love;

```
      |        |A        |        |G
```
I'm cold as a new razor blade.

```
            |        |D        |        |F♯m
```
You left when I told you I was curious;

```
      |        |E    Esus4  |E    E7
```
I never said that I was brave.

Chorus 5

Repeat Chorus 1

Verse 6

```
‖A    |        |Bm        |        |D
```
Oh, ____ you're really such a pretty one;

```
      |                |A        |        |G
```
I see you've gone and changed your name again.

```
      |                |D        |        |F♯m
```
And just when I climbed this whole mountain - side

```
            |     |E    Esus4    |E    E7
```
To wash my eye - lids _____ in the rain.

Chorus 6

```
‖A    |        |F♯m
```
Oh, so long, Marianne,

```
      |                |E    Esus4  |E    E7
```
It's time that we began to laugh   and cry

```
|E    Esus4  |E    E7        |
```
And cry   and laugh a - bout it

```
A        |Asus4    |A        |Asus4    |A        ‖
```
All again.
```
```

The Future

Words and Music by
Leonard Cohen

Am   Dm   G#°7   E7   C   F   Fm   G   F7

Intro |Am | | | ||

Verse 1

Am |
Give me back my broken night,
|**Dm** |
My mirrored room, my secret life,
|**G#°7** |**E7** |**Am** | |
It's lonely here, there's no one left to torture.
                        | |**Dm** |
Give me abso - lute control over ev'ry living soul
|**G#°7** |**E7** |**Am** | |
And lie beside me, baby, ___ that's an order!
                        | |
Give me crack and anal sex,
Dm |
Take the only tree that's left
|**G#°7** |**E7** |**Am** | |
And stuff it up the hole in your culture.
                        | |
Give me back the Berlin Wall,
Dm |
Give me Stalin and Saint Paul.
|**G#°7** |**E7** |**Am** | ||
I've seen the future, brother, it is murder.

Pre-Chorus 1

Dm | |**C** |
Things are gonna slide (Slide) in all di - rections,
        |**Dm** | |**C** |
Won't be nothing, nothing you can measure anymore.
        |**Dm** | |**F** |
The blizzard, the blizzard of the world has crossed the threshold
        |**Fm** | |**C** |
And it's overturned the order of the soul.

Chorus 1

‖ **G** |
When they said, (They said) "Repent, ___ (repent,)
| | |**Am** |
Repent." ___ (repent.) ___ I wonder what they meant.
| **G** |
When they said, (They said) "Repent, ___ (repent,)
| | |**Am** |
Repent." ___ (repent.) ___ I wonder what they meant.
| **G** |
When they said, (They said) "Repent, ___ (repent,)
| | |**Am** |
Repent." ___ (repent.) ___ I wonder what they meant.

| | | ‖

Verse 2

Am |
You don't know me from the wind,
|**Dm** | |
You never will, you never did.
G♯°7 |**E7** |**Am** |
I'm the little Jew who wrote the Bible.

| |
I've seen the nations rise and fall,
|**Dm** |
I've heard their stories, heard them all,
|**G♯°7** |**E7** |**Am** |
But love's the only engine of survival.

| |
Your servant here, he has been told
|**Dm** |
To say it clear, to say it cold.
|**G♯°7** |**E7** |**Am** |
It's over, it ain't goin' any further.

| |
And now the wheels of heaven stop,
|**Dm** |
You feel the devil's ridin' crop,
|**G♯°7** |**E7** |**Am** | ‖
Get ready for the future: it is murder.

Pre-Chorus 2   *Repeat Pre-Chorus 1*

Chorus 2

    ‖**G** |
When they said, (They said) "Repent, ___ (repent,)
     | | |**Am** |
Repent." ___ (repent.) ___ I wonder what they meant.
    |**G** |
When they said, (They said) "Repent, ___ (repent,)
     | | |**Am** |
Repent." ___ (repent.) ___ I wonder what they meant.
    |**G** |
When they said, (They said) "Repent, ___ (repent,)
     | | |**Am** | | |
Repent." ___ (repent.) ___ I wonder what they meant.

Verse 3

     ‖**Am** | | |
There'll be the breaking of the ancient Western code,
   |**Dm** | | |
Your private life will suddenly explode.
     |**Am** | |
There'll be phantoms, there'll be fires on the road,
    | |**F7** | |**E7** |
And the white man dancing.
     |**Am** | | |
You'll see your woman hanging upside down,
   |**Dm** | | |
Her features covered by her fallen gown,
    |**Am** | |
And all the lousy little poets coming 'round,
   | |**F7** | |**E7** |
Trying to sound like Charlie Manson.
      |**Am** | | | ‖
Hear the white man dancing.

Verse 4

Am | |
Give me back the Berlin Wall,
Dm | |
Give me Stalin and Saint Paul.
G♯°7 |**E7** |**Am** |
Give me Christ or give me Hiroshima.

| |
De - stroy another fetus now,
|**Dm** |
We don't like children anyhow,
|**G♯°7** |**E7** |**Am** | ‖
I've seen the future, baby: it is murder.

Pre-Chorus 3

Repeat Pre-Chorus 1

Chorus 3

‖**G** |
When they said, (They said) "Repent, ___ (repent,)
| | |**Am** |
Repent." ___ (repent.) ___ I wonder what they meant.
|**G** |
When they said, (They said) "Repent, ___ (repent,)
| | |**Am** |
Repent." ___ (repent.) ___ I wonder what they meant.
|**G** |
When they said, (They said) "Repent, ___ (repent,)
| | |**Am** |
Repent." ___ (repent.) ___ I wonder what they meant.
|**G** |
When they said, (They said) "Repent, ___ (repent,)
| | |**Am** | ‖
Repent." ___ (repent.)

Hallelujah

Words and Music by
Leonard Cohen

C   Am   F   G   E

Intro

|C |Am |C |Am

Verse 1

‖C |Am
Now, I've heard there was a secret chord
 |C |Am
That David played and it pleased the Lord,
    |F |G |C |G
But you don't really care for music, do ya?
   |C |F   G
It goes like this: the fourth, the fifth,
   |Am |F
The minor fall, the major lift,
   |G |E |Am |
The baffled King com - posing Halle - lujah.

Chorus 1

    ‖F | |Am |
Halle - lujah,   Halle - lujah,
       |F | |C |G |C |G
Halle - lujah,   Halle - lu   -   jah.

Verse 2

    ‖C |Am
Your faith was strong but you needed proof.
    |C |Am
You saw her bathing on the roof.
    |F |G |C |G
Her beauty and the moonlight over - threw ya.
    |C |F   G
She tied you to a kitchen chair.
   |Am |F
She broke your throne and she cut your hair.
    |G |E |Am |
And from your lips she drew the Halle - lujah.

Chorus 2   *Repeat Chorus 1*

Verse 3

```
    ‖C          |Am          |
You say I took the name in vain.
    C           |Am
I don't even know the name
    |F          |G           |C          |G
But if I did, well really, what's it to ya?
            |C              |F   G
There's a blaze of light in ev'ry word.
    |Am             |F
It doesn't matter which you heard,
    |G          |E           |Am          |
The holy or the broken Halle - lujah.
```

Chorus 3   *Repeat Chorus 1*

Verse 4
```
    ‖C          |Am
I did my best, it wasn't much.
    |C          |Am
I couldn't feel so I tried to touch.
    |F          |G           |C          |G
I've told the truth; I didn't come to fool ya.
    |C          |F   G
And even though it all went wrong,
    |Am             |F
I'll stand before the Lord of song
    |G          |E           |Am          |
With nothing on my tongue but Halle - lujah.
```

Chorus 4
```
        ‖F      |       |Am          |
Halle - lujah,      Halle - lujah,
        |F      |       |C   |G
Halle - lujah,      Halle - lu - jah.
        |F      |       |Am          |
Halle - lujah,      Halle - lujah,
        |F      |       |C   |G  |C   |       ‖
Halle - lujah,      Halle - lu  -     jah.
```

Hey, That's No Way to Say Goodbye

Words and Music by
Leonard Cohen

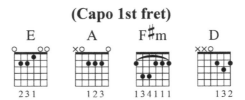

(Capo 1st fret)

Intro |E | | |

Verse 1
‖A |
I loved you in the morning, our kisses deep and warm,
|F#m |
Your hair upon the pillow like a sleepy golden storm.
|D |
Yes, many loved before us, I know that we are not new.
|A |
In city and in forest, they smiled like me and you.
|F#m |
But now it's come to distances and both of us must try.
|D |E
Your eyes are soft with sorrow.
          | |A   E | |
Hey, that's no way to say good - bye.

Verse 2

‖**A** | |
I'm not looking for another as I wander in my time.
F♯m | |
Walk me to the corner, our steps will always rhyme.
D |
You know my love goes with you as your love stays with me.
|**A** |
It's just the way it changes, like the shoreline and the sea.
|**F♯m** |
But let's not talk of love or chains and things we can't untie.
|**D** |**E**
Your eyes are soft with sorrow.
| |**A**　**E** | |
Hey, that's no way to say good - bye.

Verse 3

‖**A** |
I loved you in the morning, our kisses deep and warm,
|**F♯m** |
Your hair upon the pillow like a sleepy golden storm.
|**D** |
Yes, many loved before us, I know that we are not new.
|**A** |
In city and in forest, they smiled like me and you.
|**F♯m** |
But let's not talk of love or chains and things we can't untie.
|**D** |**E**
Your eyes are soft with sorrow.
| |**A**　**E** |**A** ‖
Hey, that's no way to say good - bye.

I'm Your Man

Words and Music by
Leonard Cohen

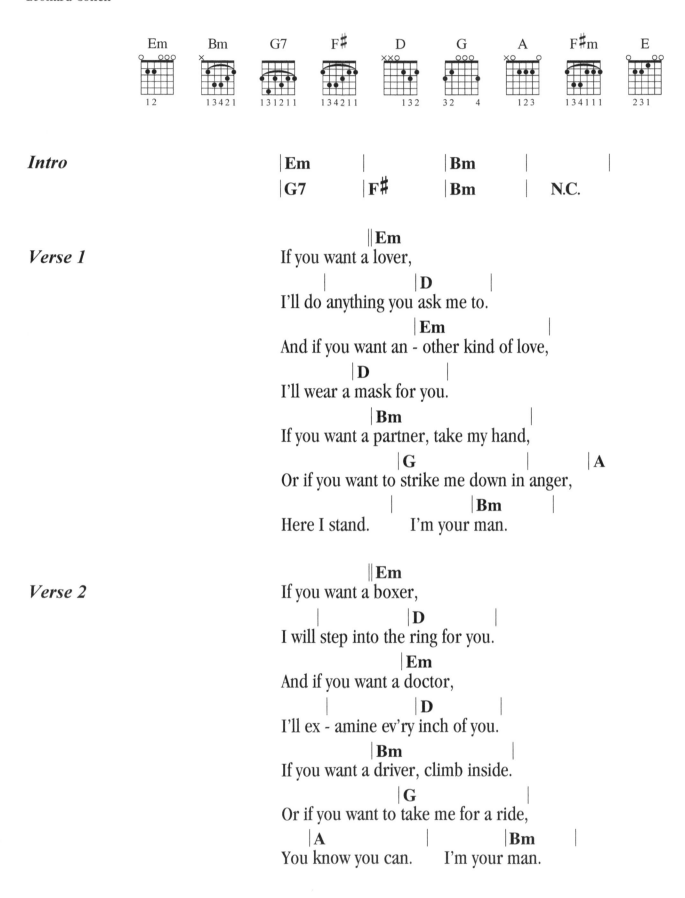

Intro

|Em | |Bm | |
|G7 |F♯ |Bm | N.C.

Verse 1

‖**Em**
If you want a lover,
        | |D |
I'll do anything you ask me to.
            |**Em** |
And if you want an - other kind of love,
        |**D** |
I'll wear a mask for you.
|**Bm** |
If you want a partner, take my hand,
            |**G** | |**A**
Or if you want to strike me down in anger,
        | |**Bm** |
Here I stand.   I'm your man.

Verse 2

‖**Em**
If you want a boxer,
        | |**D** |
I will step into the ring for you.
            |**Em** |
And if you want a doctor,
        | |**D** |
I'll ex - amine ev'ry inch of you.
        |**Bm** |
If you want a driver, climb inside.
            |**G** |
Or if you want to take me for a ride,
    |**A** | |**Bm** |
You know you can.   I'm your man.

Bridge

‖**D** |**G**
Ah, the moon's too bright, the chain's too tight,
　|**A** |**D**
The beast won't go to sleep.
　　　　|**F♯m** |
I've been running through these promises to you
　　|**Bm** |
That I made and I could not keep.
　　　　|**F♯** |
Ah, but a man never got a woman back,
　　|**Bm** |
Not by begging on his knees.
　　　|**G** |**F♯**
Or I'd crawl to you, baby, and I'd fall at your feet,
　　　|**G** |**F♯**
And I'd howl at your beauty like a dog in heat.
　　　|**G** |**E**
And I'd claw at your heart, and I'd tear at your sheet.
　　　　　　|**A** | ‖**Bm**
I'd say, please, ___ please,   I'm your man.

Interlude

Bm		**Em**	
Bm		**Em**	
D		**Bm**	
G7		**F♯**	
Bm

Verse 3

　　　　　　　　　‖**Em** |
And if you've got to sleep for a moment
　　　　　　　　|**D** |
On the road, I will steer for you.
　　　　　　　|**Em** |
And if you want to work the street alone,
　　　　|**D** |
I'll disap - pear for you.
　　　　　|**Bm** |
If you want a father for your child,
　　　　　　|**G** |
Or only want to walk with me a while
　　　|**A** | |**Bm** | ‖
Across the sand,   I'm your man.

Suzanne

Words and Music by
Leonard Cohen

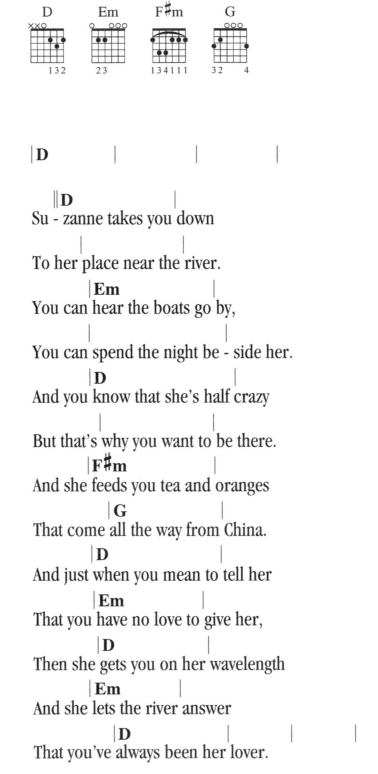

(Capo 2nd fret)

D   Em   F♯m   G

Intro

|D | | |

Verse 1

‖D |
Su - zanne takes you down

| |
To her place near the river.

|Em |
You can hear the boats go by,

| |
You can spend the night be - side her.

|D |
And you know that she's half crazy

| |
But that's why you want to be there.

|F♯m |
And she feeds you tea and oranges

|G |
That come all the way from China.

|D |
And just when you mean to tell her

|Em |
That you have no love to give her,

|D |
Then she gets you on her wavelength

|Em |
And she lets the river answer

|D | | |
That you've always been her lover.

Chorus 1

‖ **F♯m** |
And you want to travel with her,
| **G** |
And you want to travel blind,
| **D** |
And you know that she will trust you,
| **Em** |
For you've touched her perfect body
| **D** | | | |
With your mind.

Verse 2

‖ **D** |
And Jesus was a sailor
| |
When He walked upon the water.
| **Em** |
And He spent a long time watching
| |
From His lonely wooden tower.
| **D** |
And when He knew for certain
| |
Only drowning men could see Him,
| **F♯m** |
He said, "All men will be sailors then,
| **G** |
Un - til the sea shall free them."
| **D** |
But He Himself was broken
| **Em** |
Long be - fore the sky would open.
| **D** |
For - saken, almost human,
| **Em** |
He sank beneath your wisdom
| **D** | | | |
Like a stone.

Chorus 2

‖ **F♯m** |
And you want to travel with Him,
| **G** |
And you want to travel blind,
| **D** |
And you think maybe you'll trust Him,
| **Em** |
For He's touched your perfect body
| **D** | | | |
With His mind.

Verse 3

    ‖**D** |

Now, Su - zanne takes your hand

    | |

And she leads you to the river.

  |**Em** |

She is wearing rags and feathers

     | |

From sal - vation army counters.

   |**D** |

And the sun pours down like honey

    | |

On our lady of the harbor,

  |**F♯m** |

And she shows you where to look

     |**G** |

Among the garbage and the flowers.

    |**D** |

There are heroes in the seaweed.

    |**Em** |

There are children in the morning.

    |**D** |

They are leaning out for love,

      |**Em** |

And they will lean that way for - ever

    |**D** | | |

While Su - zanne holds the mirror.

Chorus 3

    ‖**F♯m** |

And you want to travel with her,

   |**G** |

And you want to travel blind,

   |**D** |

And you know you can trust her,

   |**Em** |

For she's touched your perfect body

   |**D** | | | ‖

With her mind.

A Thousand Kisses Deep

Words and Music by
Leonard Cohen and Sharon Robinson

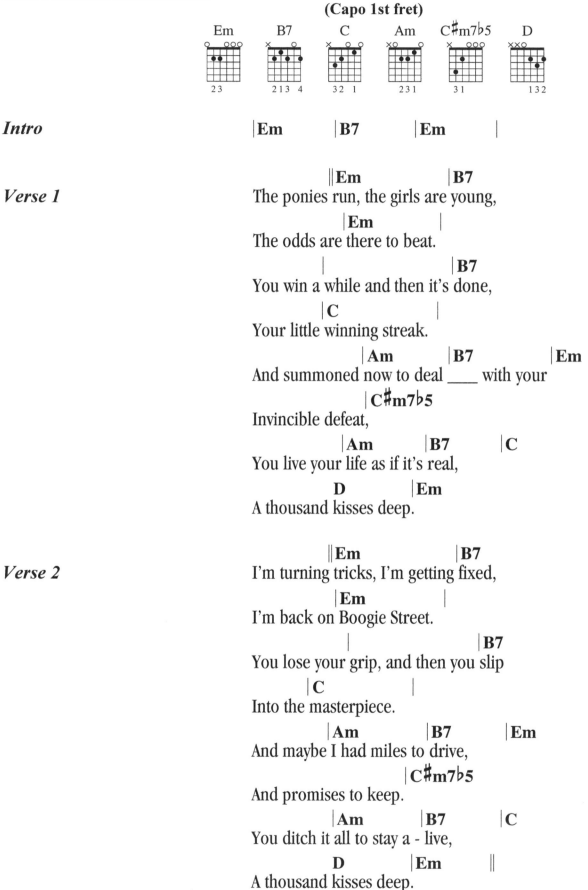

(Capo 1st fret)

Em   B7   C   Am   C#m7b5   D

Intro

|Em |B7 |Em |

Verse 1

‖Em |B7
The ponies run, the girls are young,
|Em |
The odds are there to beat.
| |B7
You win a while and then it's done,
|C |
Your little winning streak.
            |Am |B7 |Em
And summoned now to deal ___ with your
        |C#m7b5
Invincible defeat,
        |Am |B7 |C
You live your life as if it's real,
        D |Em
A thousand kisses deep.

Verse 2

‖Em |B7
I'm turning tricks, I'm getting fixed,
|Em |
I'm back on Boogie Street.
| |B7
You lose your grip, and then you slip
|C |
Into the masterpiece.
        |Am |B7 |Em
And maybe I had miles to drive,
            |C#m7b5
And promises to keep.
        |Am |B7 |C
You ditch it all to stay a - live,
        D |Em   ‖
A thousand kisses deep.

Interlude 1 |Em |B7 |Em | | |
          | |B7 |C |

Chorus 1

‖Am |B7 |Em
And sometimes when the night is slow,
|C♯m7♭5
The wretched and the meek,
|Am |B7 |C
We gather up our hearts and go
D |Em
A thousand kisses deep.

Verse 3

‖Em |B7
Confined to sex we pressed a - gainst
|Em |
The limits of the sea.
| |B7 |C
I saw there were no oceans ___ left
|
For scavengers like me.
|Am |B7 |Em
I made it to the forward deck,
|C♯m7♭5
I blessed our remnant fleet,
|Am |B7 |C
And then con - sented to be wrecked
D |Em
A thousand kisses deep.

Verse 4

```
        ‖Em              |B7
I'm turning tricks, I'm getting fixed,
         |Em              |
I'm back on Boogie Street.
         |                |B7
I guess they won't exchange the gifts
              |C              |
That you were meant to keep.
         |Am            |B7         |Em
And quiet is the thought of you,
                         |C♯m7♭5
The file on you complete,
              |Am        |B7         |C
Except what we forgot to do
            D        |Em
A thousand kisses deep.
```

Interlude 2   *Repeat Interlude 1*

Chorus 2   *Repeat Chorus 1*

Verse 5

```
          ‖Em              |B7
The ponies run, the girls are young,
              |Em              |
The odds are there to beat.
         |                |B7
You win a while and then it's done,
              |C              |
Your little winning streak.
              |Am        |B7         |Em
And summoned now to deal ___ with your
              |C♯m7♭5
Invincible defeat,
              |Am        |B7         |C
You live your life as if it's real,
            D        |Em          ‖
A thousand kisses deep.
```

Waiting for the Miracle

Words and Music by
Leonard Cohen and Sharon Robinson

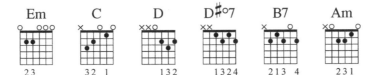

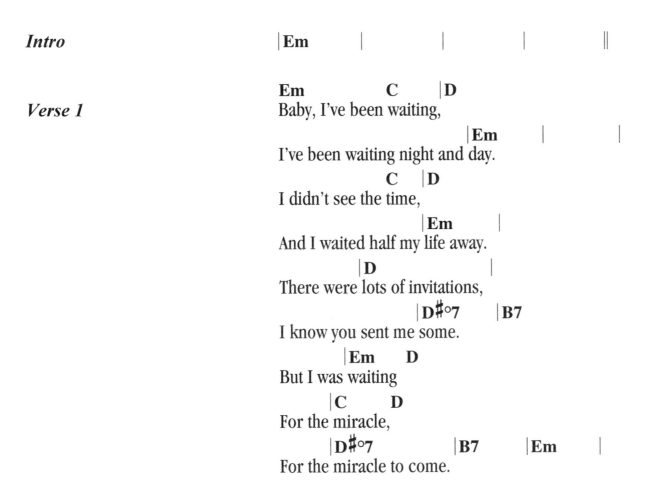

Intro

|Em | | | ||

Verse 1

Em   C |D
Baby, I've been waiting,
                              |Em | |
I've been waiting night and day.
                    C |D
I didn't see the time,
                              |Em |
And I waited half my life away.
              |D |
There were lots of invitations,
                    |D#°7 |B7
I know you sent me some.
              |Em   D
But I was waiting
          |C   D
For the miracle,
          |D#°7 |B7 |Em |
For the miracle to come.

Verse 2

```
        ‖Em            C        |D
I know you really love me,
                |Em          |            |
But, you see, my hands were tied.
                           C        |D
And I know it must have hurt you,
                        |Em        |
It must have hurt your pride
            |D                      |
To have to stand beneath my window
                          |D♯○7      |B7
With your bugle and your drum.
                        |Em     D
And me, I'm up there waiting
        |C        D
For the miracle,
        |D♯○7              |B7        |Em        |
For the miracle to come.
```

Verse 3

```
            ‖Em            C     |D
Yeah, I don't believe you'd like it,
                    |Em        |            |
You wouldn't like it here.
                       C        |D
There ain't no enter - tainment,
                        |Em        |
And the judgments are severe.
        |D                      |
The Maestro says it's Mozart,
                |D♯○7        |B7
But it sounds like bubble gum
            |Em     D
When you're waiting
        |C        D
For the miracle,
        |D♯○7              |B7        |Em        |            ‖
For the miracle to come.
```

Chorus 1

```
Am                 |
Waiting for the miracle,
      |Em            |            |B7
There's nothin' left to do.
                           |
I haven't been this happy
             |Em           |
Since the end of World War Two.
                  |Am                               |
Nothin' left to do when you know that you've been taken,
                  |Em                        |
Nothin' left to do when you're begging for a crumb.
                  |C                   |            |
Nothin' left to do when you've got to go on waiting,
D#°7                      |B7         |            |
Waiting for the miracle to come.
```

Verse 4

```
           ||Em              C      |D
Yeah, I dreamed about you, baby,
                    |Em          |            |
It was just the other night.
                 C        |D
Most of you was naked,
                          |Em          |
Ah, but some of you was light.
   |D                        |
The sands of time were falling
                          |D#°7       |B7
From your fingers and your thumb,
             |Em       D
And you were waiting
         |C         D
For the miracle,
         |D#°7              |B7        |Em          |
For the miracle to come.
```

Verse 5

‖**Em**   **C** |**D**
Yeah baby, let's get married,

     |**Em** | |
We've been alone too long.

    C |**D**
Let's be alone to - gether,

     |**Em** |
Let's see if we're that strong.

|**D** |
Yeah, let's do somethin' crazy,

     |**D♯°7** |**B7**
Somethin' absolutely wrong

    |**Em**   **D**
While we are waiting

 |**C**   **D**
For the miracle,

  |**D♯°7** |**B7** |**Em** |
For the miracle to come.

Chorus 2

      ‖ **Am** |
Nothin' left to do when you know you've been taken,

     |**Em** |
Nothin' left to do when you're begging for a crumb.

    |**C** | |
Nothin' left to do when you've got to go on waiting,

D♯°7 |**B7** | |
Waiting for the miracle to come.

Verse 6

     ‖**Em**   **C** |**D**
When you've fallen on the highway,

    |**Em** |
And you're lying in the rain,

 | **C** |**D**
And they ask you how you're doing,

      |**Em** |
Of course, you say you can't com - plain.

 |**D** |
If you're squeezed for information,

       |**D♯°7** |**B7**
That's when you've got to play it dumb.

       |**Em**   **D**
You just say you're out there waiting

 |**C**   **D**
For the miracle,

 |**D♯°7** |**B7** |**Em** | ‖
For the miracle to come.

STRUM & SING

The Strum & Sing series for guitar and ukulele provides an unplugged and pared-down approach to your favorite songs – just the chords and the lyrics, with nothing fancy. These easy-to-play arrangements are designed for both aspiring and professional musicians.

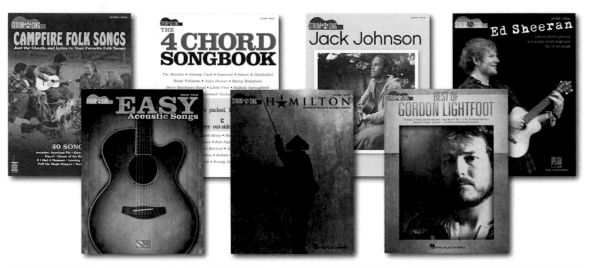

GUITAR

Acoustic Classics
00191891 ....$16.99

Adele
00159855 ....$12.99

Sara Bareilles
00102354 ....$12.99

The Beatles
00172234 ....$17.99

Blues
00159335 ....$12.99

Zac Brown Band
02501620 ....$19.99

Colbie Caillat
02501725 ....$14.99

Campfire Folk Songs
02500686 ....$15.99

Chart Hits of 2014-2015
00142554 ....$12.99

Chart Hits of 2015-2016
00156248 ....$12.99

Best of Kenny Chesney
00142457 ....$14.99

Christmas Carols
00348351 ....$14.99

Christmas Songs
00171332 ....$14.99

Kelly Clarkson
00146384 ....$14.99

Leonard Cohen
00265489 ....$16.99

Dear Evan Hansen
00295108 ....$16.99

John Denver Collection
02500632 ....$17.99

Disney
00233900 ....$17.99

Eagles
00157994 ....$14.99

Easy Acoustic Songs
00125478 ....$19.99

Billie Eilish
00363094 ....$14.99

The Five-Chord Songbook
02501718 ....$14.99

Folk Rock Favorites
02501669 ....$16.99

Folk Songs
02501482 ....$15.99

The Four-Chord Country Songbook
00114936 ....$16.99

The Four Chord Songbook
02501533 ....$14.99

Four Chord Songs
00249581 ....$16.99

The Greatest Showman
00278383 ....$14.99

Hamilton
00217116 ....$15.99

Jack Johnson
02500858 ....$19.99

Robert Johnson
00191890 ....$12.99

Carole King
00115243 ....$10.99

Best of Gordon Lightfoot
00139393 ....$15.99

John Mayer
02501636 ....$19.99

The Most Requested Songs
02501748 ....$19.99

Jason Mraz
02501452 ....$14.99

**Tom Petty –
Wildflowers & All the Rest**
00362682 ....$14.99

Elvis Presley
00198890 ....$12.99

Queen
00218578 ....$12.99

Rock Around the Clock
00103625 ....$12.99

Rock Ballads
02500872 ....$12.99

Rocketman
00300469 ....$17.99

Ed Sheeran
00152016 ....$14.99

The Six-Chord Songbook
02502277 ....$17.99

Chris Stapleton
00362625 ....$19.99

Cat Stevens
00116827 ....$17.99

Taylor Swift
01191699 ....$19.99

The Three-Chord Songbook
00211634 ....$14.99

Top Christian Hits
00156331 ....$12.99

Top Hits of 2016
00194288 ....$12.99

The Who
00103667 ....$12.99

Yesterday
00301629 ....$14.99

Neil Young – Greatest Hits
00138270 ....$16.99

UKULELE

The Beatles
00233899 ....$16.99

Colbie Caillat
02501731 ....$10.99

Coffeehouse Songs
00138238 ....$14.99

John Denver
02501694 ....$17.99

The 4-Chord Ukulele Songbook
00114331 ....$16.99

Jack Johnson
02501702 ....$19.99

John Mayer
02501706 ....$10.99

The Most Requested Songs
02501453 ....$15.99

Pop Songs for Kids
00284415 ....$17.99

Sing-Along Songs
02501710 ....$17.99

HAL•LEONARD®

halleonard.com
Visit our website to see full song lists
or order from your favorite retailer.

*Prices, contents and availability
subject to change without notice.*

Guitar Chord Songbooks

Each 6" x 9" book includes complete lyrics, chord symbols, and guitar chord diagrams.

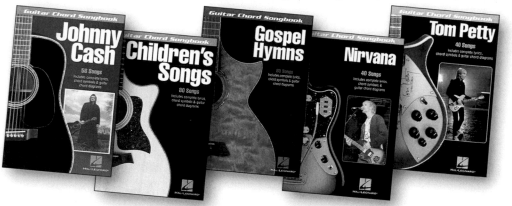

Acoustic Hits
00701787 . . . . $14.99

Acoustic Rock
00699540 . . . . $22.99

Alabama
00699914 . . . . $14.95

The Beach Boys
00699566 . . . . $19.99

Bluegrass
00702585 . . . . $14.99

Johnny Cash
00699648 . . . . $19.99

Children's Songs
00699539 . . . . $17.99

Christmas Carols
00699536 . . . . $14.99

Christmas Songs
00119911 . . . . $14.99

Eric Clapton
00699567 . . . . $19.99

Classic Rock
00699598 . . . . $20.99

Coffeehouse Hits
00703318 . . . . $14.99

Country
00699534 . . . . $17.99

Country Favorites
00700609 . . . . $14.99

Country Hits
00140859 . . . . $14.99

Country Standards
00700608 . . . . $12.95

Cowboy Songs
00699636 . . . . $19.99

Creedence Clearwater Revival
00701786 . . . . $16.99

Jim Croce
00148087 . . . . $14.99

Crosby, Stills & Nash
00701609 . . . . $17.99

John Denver
02501697 . . . . $19.99

Neil Diamond
00700606 . . . . $22.99

Disney – 2nd Edition
00295786 . . . . $19.99

The Doors
00699888 . . . . $22.99

Eagles
00122917 . . . . $19.99

Early Rock
00699916 . . . . $14.99

Folksongs
00699541 . . . . $16.99

Folk Pop Rock
00699651 . . . . $17.99

40 Easy Strumming Songs
00115972 . . . . $16.99

Four Chord Songs
00701611 . . . . $16.99

Glee
00702501 . . . . $14.99

Gospel Hymns
00700463 . . . . $16.99

Grateful Dead
00139461 . . . . $17.99

Green Day
00103074 . . . . $17.99

Irish Songs
00701044 . . . . $16.99

Michael Jackson
00137847 . . . . $14.99

Billy Joel
00699632 . . . . $22.99

Elton John
00699732 . . . . $17.99

Ray LaMontagne
00130337 . . . . $12.99

Latin Songs
00700973 . . . . $14.99

Love Songs
00701043 . . . . $14.99

Bob Marley
00701704 . . . . $17.99

Bruno Mars
00125332 . . . . $12.99

Paul McCartney
00385035 . . . . $19.99

Steve Miller
00701146 . . . . $12.99

Modern Worship
00701801 . . . . $19.99

Motown
00699734 . . . . $19.99

Willie Nelson
00148273 . . . . $17.99

Nirvana
00699762 . . . . $17.99

Roy Orbison
00699752 . . . . $19.99

Peter, Paul & Mary
00103013 . . . . $19.99

Tom Petty
00699883 . . . . $17.99

Pink Floyd
00139116 . . . . $17.99

Pop/Rock
00699538 . . . . $19.99

Praise & Worship
00699634 . . . . $14.99

Elvis Presley
00699633 . . . . $17.99

Queen
00702395 . . . . $17.99

Red Hot Chili Peppers
00699710 . . . . $24.99

The Rolling Stones
00137716 . . . . $19.99

Bob Seger
00701147 . . . . $16.99

Carly Simon
00121011 . . . . $14.99

Sting
00699921 . . . . $24.99

Three Chord Acoustic Songs
00123860 . . . . $16.99

Three Chord Songs
00699720 . . . . $17.99

Two-Chord Songs
00119236 . . . . $16.99

U2
00137744 . . . . $19.99

Hank Williams
00700607 . . . . $16.99

Stevie Wonder
00120862 . . . . $14.99

Prices and availability subject to change without notice.

HAL•LEONARD®
Visit Hal Leonard online at **www.halleonard.com**

AUTHENTIC CHORDS • ORIGINAL KEYS • COMPLETE SONGS

The *Strum It* series lets players strum the chords and sing along with their favorite hits. Each song has been selected because it can be played with regular open chords, barre chords, or other moveable chord types. Guitarists can simply play the rhythm, or play and sing along through the entire song. All songs are shown in their original keys complete with chords, strum patterns, melody and lyrics. Wherever possible, the chord voicings from the recorded versions are notated.

THE BEACH BOYS' GREATEST HITS
00699357.................................. $12.95

THE BEATLES FAVORITES
00699249..................................$15.99

VERY BEST OF JOHNNY CASH
00699514..................................$14.99

CELTIC GUITAR SONGBOOK
00699265..................................$12.99

CHRISTMAS SONGS FOR GUITAR
00699247..................................$10.95

CHRISTMAS SONGS WITH 3 CHORDS
00699487....................................$9.99

VERY BEST OF ERIC CLAPTON
00699560..................................$12.95

JIM CROCE – CLASSIC HITS
00699269..................................$10.95

DISNEY FAVORITES
00699171..................................$14.99

MELISSA ETHERIDGE GREATEST HITS
00699518..................................$12.99

FAVORITE SONGS WITH 3 CHORDS
00699112..................................$10.99

FAVORITE SONGS WITH 4 CHORDS
00699270....................................$8.95

FIRESIDE SING-ALONG
00699273..................................$12.99

FOLK FAVORITES
00699517....................................$8.95

THE GUITAR STRUMMERS' ROCK SONGBOOK
00701678..................................$14.99

BEST OF WOODY GUTHRIE
00699496..................................$12.95

JOHN HIATT COLLECTION
00699398..................................$17.99

THE VERY BEST OF BOB MARLEY
00699524..................................$14.99

A MERRY CHRISTMAS SONGBOOK
00699211..................................$10.99

MORE FAVORITE SONGS WITH 3 CHORDS
00699532....................................$9.99

THE VERY BEST OF TOM PETTY
00699336..................................$15.99

BEST OF GEORGE STRAIT
00699235..................................$16.99

TAYLOR SWIFT FOR ACOUSTIC GUITAR
00109717..................................$16.99

BEST OF HANK WILLIAMS JR.
00699224..................................$16.99

Visit Hal Leonard online at
www.halleonard.com

Prices, contents & availability
subject to change without notice.